Presented to

_____

By

_____

On

_____

My Child

Written by

Steven H. Waller

Illustrated by

Kathy Fincher

Regina Press

Dedication

This edition of *My Child* is dedicated to the memory of Tim Miller. The love between a parent and child is forever. May God continue to comfort and sustain the Miller family in the years to come.

The Regina Press
10 Hub Drive
Melville, New York 11747
www.reginapress.com

Copyright © 2008 by the Regina Press. All rights reserved.
Text copyright Steven H. Waller © 2008.
Artwork copyright Kathy Fincher © 2008.

No part of this book may be reproduced in any form without expressed permission from the publisher.

Printed in China.

ISBN 9780882711720

The Regina Press and Steven H. Waller would like to acknowledge Pat Fieser. It is because of her support and encouragement that the message of *My Child* has been shared with so many people, and this book has been published.

Introduction

We all search for words to express how we feel about special people in our lives, especially our children. Hopefully the words and images in this book will help do this for parents. If there is a purpose for this book, it would be to help keep open the doors of love and communication for parents and children.

I would like to acknowledge my parents, who first opened the doors of love for me. Because I experienced their love, I was able to do the same with my wife for our children, their spouses and our grandchildren. These are the people I share love with on a daily basis.

This version is an adaptation of the original *My Child*, which appears at the end of the book. It is a loving way for parents to share heartfelt moments with their younger children.

Steven H. Waller

My Child

Know this...
There is not
a more genuine
or important message
I, as your parent,
have to offer.
I love you
and will always love you.

My Child

I will try to show you

by my words

and actions

this love,

but realize

I may fall short

of this goal

at times.

My Chi...

I will,

to the best of my ability,

with the work of my body,

the limits of my mind

and strength of my soul,

try to give you love,

shelter and food.

My Child

I will try to give you

as much of my time

as possible

in this hectic,

hurried world.

My Chi...

I will try
to give you
fun and
laughter.

My Child

I will try

to give you

the safety

and protection

you have a right to

and I have an

obligation to give.

My Child

I will try

to let you know

about life's unpleasantries

without scaring you

too much.

I will try to give you

as much trust as possible

in an apparently

untrusting world.

My Child

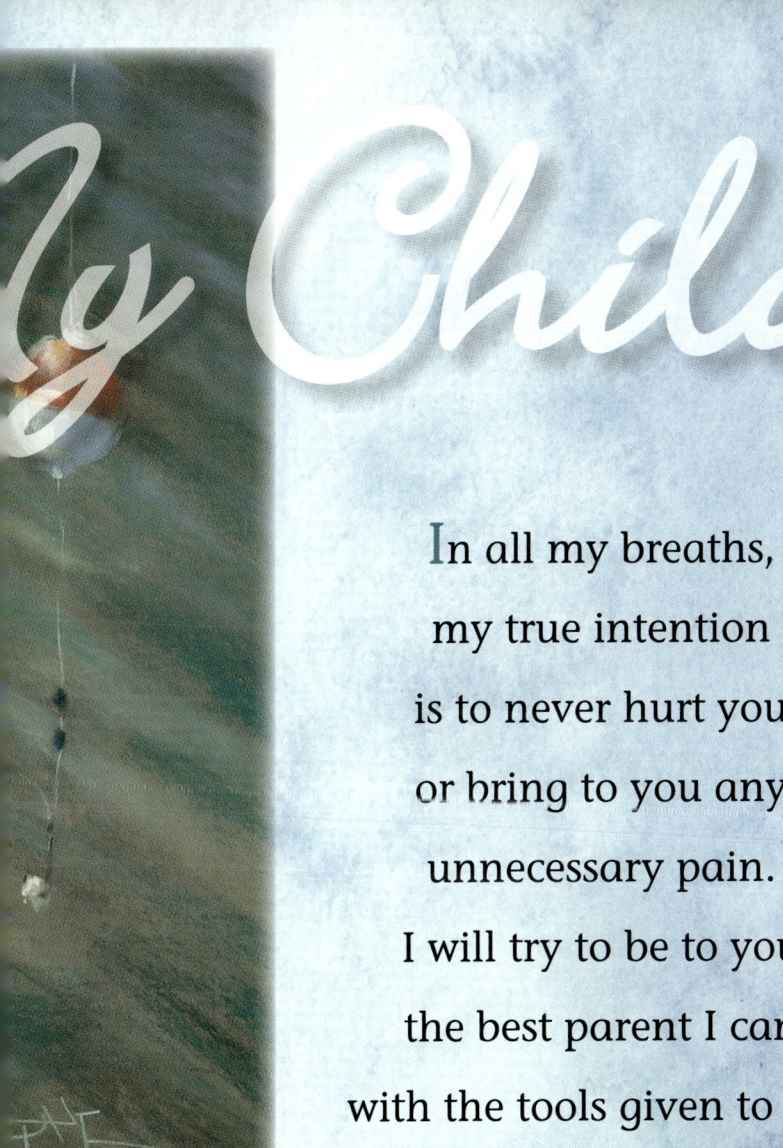

In all my breaths,
my true intention
is to never hurt you
or bring to you any
unnecessary pain.
I will try to be to you
the best parent I can
with the tools given to me.

My Child

I want you to know
that for any times
I will hurt you,
disappoint you,
or let you down,
knowingly or
unknowingly,
I am sorry.

My Child

Thank you for the
pleasures and treasures
you give and will give to me,
both now and
in the years to come.
There is nothing you have done
or will ever do
that will take away
my unconditional love
for you.

My Child

Always and now,

in my eyes,

heart and soul,

know you are to me

the most beautiful bud,

the loveliest bloom,

and the most perfect flower.

My Child

I have loved you

from the day

you were born...

I love you

with every breath

you take...

I will love you...

forever.

My Child
Adapted Version

Know this... There is not a more genuine or important message I, as your parent, have to offer. I love you and will always love you.

I will try to show you by my words and actions this love, but realize I may fall short of this goal at times.

I will, to the best of my ability, with the work of my body, the limits of my mind and strength of my soul, try to give you love, shelter and food.

I will try to give you as much of my time as possible in this hectic, hurried world. I will try to give you fun and laughter.

I will try to give you the safety and protection you have a right to and I have an obligation to give.

I will try to let you know about life's unpleasantries
without scaring you too much. I will try to give
you as much trust as possible in an apparently
untrusting world.

In all my breaths, my true intention is to never
hurt you or bring to you any unnecessary pain.
I will try to be to you the best parent I can
with the tools given to me.

I want you to know that for any times
I will hurt you, disappoint you, or let you down,
knowingly or unknowingly, I am sorry.

Thank you for the pleasures and treasures you give
and will give to me, both now and in the years to
come. There is nothing you have done or
will ever do that will take away
my unconditional love for you.

Always and now, in my eyes, heart and soul, know
you are to me the most beautiful bud, the loveliest
bloom, and the most perfect flower.

I have loved you from the day you were born...
I love you with every breath you take...
I will love you... forever.

My Child
Original Version

Know this... There is not a more genuine or important message I, as your parent, have to offer. I love you and have always loved you.

I have tried to show you by my words and actions this love, but realize I may have fallen short of this goal at times.

I have, to the best of my ability, with the work of my body, the limits of my mind and strength of my soul, tried to give you as much of my time as possible in this hectic, hurried world. I have tried to give you fun and laughter. I have tried to give you the safety and protection you have aright to and I have an obligation to give.

I have tried to let you know about life's unpleasentries without scaring you too much. I have tried to give you as much trust as possible in an apparent untrusting world.

In all my breaths, my true intention has never been to hurt you or bring to you any unnecessary pain. I have tried to be to you the best parent I could with the tools given to me.

I want you to know that for any times I have hurt you, disappointed you, or let you down, knowingly or unknowingly, I am sorry for my shortcomings and the mistakes I made that caused you any pain. For this I ask your forgiveness, only when and if you are willing to give it.

Thank you for the pleasures and treasures you have given me, both deserved and not. There has never been anything you have done that has taken away my unconditional love for you.

Always and now, in my eyes, heart and soul, you are to me the most beautiful bud, the loveliest bloom, and the most perfect flower.

I have loved you from the day you were born...
I love you with every breath you take...
I will love you... forever.